# • LUNCH-HOUR •
# Embroidery
## 130 PLAYFUL MOTIFS FROM A TO Z

## Martingale®
*Create with Confidence*

Lunch-Hour Embroidery: 130 Playful Motifs from A to Z
© 2017 by Martingale & Company®

Martingale®
19021 120th Ave. NE, Ste. 102
Bothell, WA 98011-9511 USA
ShopMartingale.com

Printed in China
22 21 20 19 18 17          8 7 6 5 4 3 2 1

Library of Congress Cataloging-in-Publication Data
is available upon request.

ISBN: 978-1-60468-898-6

## MISSION STATEMENT

We empower makers who use fabric and yarn
to make life more enjoyable.

## CREDITS

PUBLISHER AND
CHIEF VISIONARY OFFICER
Jennifer Erbe Keltner

CONTENT DIRECTOR
Karen Costello Soltys

DESIGN MANAGER
Adrienne Smitke

MANAGING EDITOR
Tina Cook

PRODUCTION MANAGER
Regina Girard

ACQUISITIONS EDITOR
Karen M. Burns

PHOTOGRAPHER
Brent Kane

TECHNICAL WRITER
Karen Bolesta

PATTERN ILLUSTRATIONS
Adrienne Smitke

PATTERN EMBROIDERY
Cathy Valentine

# Contents

# Introduction

**Who doesn't want to sneak in a few stitches over a lunch hour?** These embroidery designs are so fast and fun that you'll want to start a new project every single day! (Are you inspired to stitch more than one a day? So are we!)

Discover how 10 simple embroidery stitches, from the easygoing chain stitch to the elegant French knot, combine to create motifs you can use for oodles of great projects. Check out the happy hedgehog on page 27 and his effortless running-stitch outlines and long-stitch spines—what a cutie! And you won't be able to resist the lovely llamas on page 35, with their French knot garlands and patterned blankets.

Teach yourself these embroidery stitches in minutes. Pull out a woven cotton fabric from your stash, cut a 12" square, and arrange and practice each stitch 5 to 10 times using your favorite floss colors. You can hang your stylish sampler as inspiration. The simple nature of the stitches means you'll perfect your stitching technique in your first lunch hour of embroidery.

Getting started involves just a few supplies you may have already in your craft cabinet, such as embroidery floss and fabric, and a few tools like a hoop, embroidery needles, and sharp scissors. If you're trying embroidery as a first-timer and need to buy supplies, you'll find that for under $10 you can be on your way to a very creative lunch hour. Why not ask a friend to join in?

All your favorite motifs are included, from donuts to dinosaurs and raccoons to robots and rockets. By combining three or four embroidery stitches per motif, you'll add texture and movement to these cute patterns. With more than 75 designs and a cap-and-lowercase alphabet, you can pair motifs and words for a modern crafty look. Try stitching *D is for Donuts* and scattering donut motifs on an apron. What a cute birthday gift for your favorite baker! How about the needles and thimble motif on a pincushion? Combine the octopus, anchor, and whale on a T-shirt for a special toddler in your life. Or embroider *Hello, Sunshine* with the cheerful yellow crayon on a place mat to greet the sleepyheads in your household each morning! For more fun ideas, see the photos, opposite.

## Wishing you a very happy embroidery lunch hour!

# Embroidery Basics

Gather your supplies or shop for inexpensive embroidery supplies at your local craft store, fabric shop, or online sites, and start having fun with embroidery!

## FABRICS

You can embroider designs on almost any woven fabric, including cotton and cotton blends, linen, muslin, and Osnaburg. Nonwoven fabrics may need a stabilizer to ensure stitches stay even.

All of the designs in the A to Z section were stitched on a white cotton-linen blend. The embroidered designs on page 4 accent a variety of fun purchased items, from a kitchen towel to a zippered bag. Prewash and press fabrics if your embroidery motif will be used in a project that will need laundering, such as clothing or table linens.

## WASH YOUR HANDS

*Wash (and dry) your hands often as you stitch to avoid staining your embroidery fabric with sweat or body oils. If you do find a stain, wash the area with a mild dishwashing liquid (but spot-test first!).*

## EMBROIDERY FLOSS

Embroidery floss is a loosely twisted, 6-stranded cotton (or other fiber) thread that can be separated into individual strands. Skeins contain about 8 yards of floss and are available in hundreds of colors.

If you'd like to experiment with a thicker thread, try pearl cotton. It has a silky sheen and is available in sizes 3 (thicker) and 5 (thinner) for embroidery.

## EMBROIDERY NEEDLES

There are three features you'll want in an embroidery needle: a medium length for good control; a sharp point to pierce tightly woven fabrics; and a long eye to allow for multiple floss strands. Needle sizes range from 1 (large) to 12 (small), with sizes 7 and 9 being the most popular for embroidery.

Treat yourself to new needles when you start a project; previously used needles can have burrs, rust, or dull spots that can snag or damage your embroidery fabric as you pull the needle through. For larger projects, change needles often to keep the needle gliding effortlessly through the embroidery fabric as you stitch.

## EMBROIDERY SCISSORS

While you can use craft or sewing scissors for embroidery, small embroidery scissors with a sharp point will make snipping threads much more precise. Some thread artists prefer curved-tip blades to straight blades because the curve allows you to work over and around other stitches. Visit a store to sample the embroidery-scissors models available and test-fit the finger holes for size and comfort.

## EMBROIDERY HOOPS

Hoops are made of bamboo, wood, and plastic and come in many sizes. Most hoops consist of two round or oval frames, nestled inside one another, with a tension screw or spring to secure the outer ring in place over the embroidery fabric. For the designs in this book, choose a round or oval hoop that is 5" to 7" in diameter.

To use a hoop, place the inner ring on a flat surface, center the fabric area to be stitched over the ring, then place the outer ring in place, gently pulling the fabric so it is smooth and taut; tighten the tension screw. Some embroiderers prefer that the fabric be drum tight; others prefer to have some give in the fabric tension. Experiment with each new project to find what works best for you.

Do you need to use a hoop at all? Your fabric needs to have some tension as you work, which a hoop provides. Without a hoop, you may find the fabric background puckers between embroidered areas. Experienced embroiderers may choose to stitch without a hoop because they are able to create tension with their fingers as they hold the fabric.

## REMOVE THE HOOP

*Take your embroidery out of the hoop after each stitching session to avoid distorting the fabric weave permanently.*

## DESIGN TRANSFER TOOLS

Depending on the transfer method you use, you may need one or more of the following tools: pencil, water-soluble marker, tracing paper, black marker, heat-transfer pen, laser printer, and Sulky Sticky Fabri-Solvy wash-away stabilizer.

## TRANSFERRING DESIGNS TO FABRIC

There are a number of ways to transfer these embroidery designs to your project fabric. Research online tutorials for details about each method.

**Tracing with a light source.** For thin or light-colored fabrics, trace the design onto tissue or copy paper, then darken (but don't thicken) the traced lines with a fine-point black marker. Place your fabric on top of the traced design and lightly trace the design lines with a pencil or water-erasable marker. If you have trouble seeing the design lines through the fabric, you can tape the design paper and fabric to a window so that the light source makes the lines visible. And if you have a lightbox, transferring designs is a snap, even with dark fabrics.

**Heat-transfer pencil.** Similar to the technique above, you'll trace the motif onto tracing or copy paper with a special heat-transfer pencil. (For asymmetrical or one-way designs, you'll need to reverse the design before you trace it.) Flip over the tracing paper so that the image side is down, place it on your project fabric, and press with dry heat until the image transfers.

**Sulky Sticky Fabri-Solvy wash-away stabilizer.** A water-soluble stabilizer is perfect for dark fabrics (and all other fabrics, too) and allows you to trace the design and adhere it right on top of the embroidery fabric. These stabilizers are thin and have an adhesive back that you can reposition. Embroider right through the stabilizer, then dissolve it in warm water, following the manufacturer's directions. You can even run sheets of stabilizer through your laser printer!

# Embroidery Stitches

You'll use only 10 stitches to create all the cute motifs featured. These tips will set you up for embroidery success.

**BACKSTITCH.** Use a backstitch for straight or angular lines. It replicates the look of machine stitching and helps to contain an area of stitches or define open space.

**CHAIN STITCH.** This decorative stitch is a perfect way to create a heavier-weight line with texture.

**CROSS-STITCH.** A cross-stitch is two stitches that form an X. Simple as that. Just be sure to keep the two stitch lengths the same. To make a snowflake, stitch two cross-stitches resting atop one another.

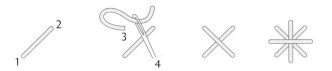

**FRENCH KNOT.** Practice French knots about 10 times and you'll be a pro. The trick is to keep slight tension on the thread emerging from the hole as you wrap, and to reinsert the needle into the fabric at least one woven thread away from where it emerged. Wrapping the thread two times works for most motifs, but wrap a third time for a bigger knot.

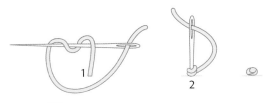

Wrap twice.

**LAZY DAISY.** A stand-alone version of the chain stitch, lazy daisy forms charming flowers when grouped in a circle.

**LONG STITCH.** It is what it says—a LOOONG stitch that's ideal for adding drama, movement, and visual volume to a design.

**RUNNING STITCH.** This stitch is adaptable to the project's needs—short and compact or long and ongoing. Make your stitches even, no matter the stitch length you choose. Or try varying stitch size and spacing for a different effect.

**SATIN STITCH.** This stitch is like using crayons to fill in a space—you'll make stitch after stitch right next to each other. To create a smoother edge, use a stem stitch or backstitch around the perimeter before filling in with satin stitching.

Backstitch around the shape first for a smoother edge.

**STEM STITCH.** Stem stitch is ideal for curved lines and tight circles because the technique allows for slants. For a smoother stem stitch, keep the loose thread above (or to the outside of the curve of) your work as you make each new stitch.

**STIPPLE STITCH.** Quilters love to use this stitch to fill space, and now embroiderers will love it, too. It adds texture and movement and fills in a shape without being as dense as a satin stitch.

Stitch sparsely or densely to create different textures.

## THE KEY TO IT ALL

Below is a key to the specific stitches used in each motif. A thin solid line indicates the stem stitch, a dashed line means use a running stitch, and so on.

## PATTERN STITCH KEY

| | |
|---|---|
| BACKSTITCH | LONG STITCH |
| CHAIN STITCH | RUNNING STITCH |
| CROSS-STITCH | SATIN STITCH |
| FRENCH KNOT | STEM STITCH |
| LAZY DAISY | STIPPLE STITCH |

## COLOR CLUES

The floss used in this book is DMC brand. If you'd like to match your stitching to the versions in the book, refer to the photo at right for the exact color numbers. However, you should feel free to use whatever colors strike your fancy!

**DMC#**

552
3837
915
498
817
351
352
945
838
975
783
444
166
581
895
163
563
3850
3808
3810
598
824
798
158
3799
414
3072

F f

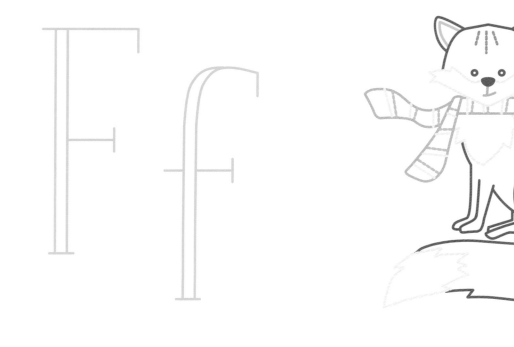

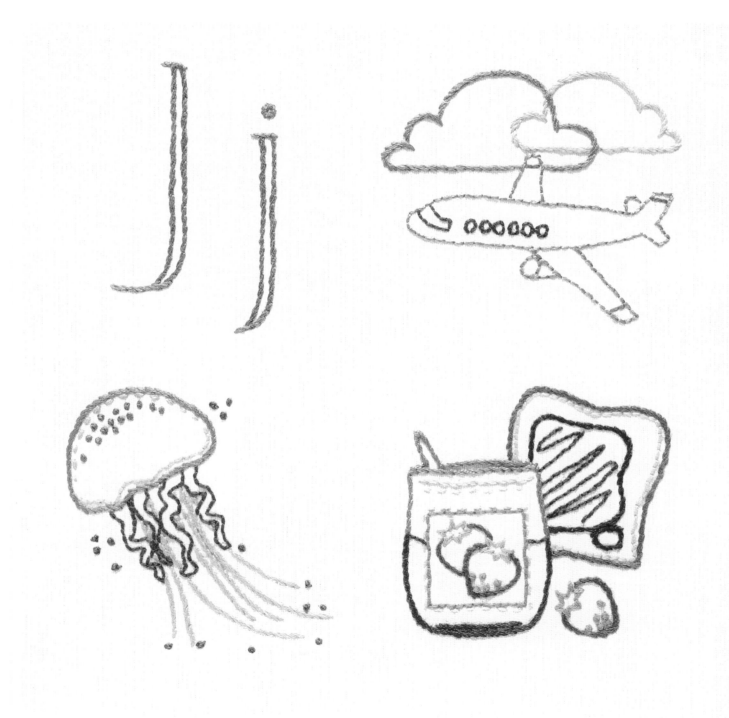

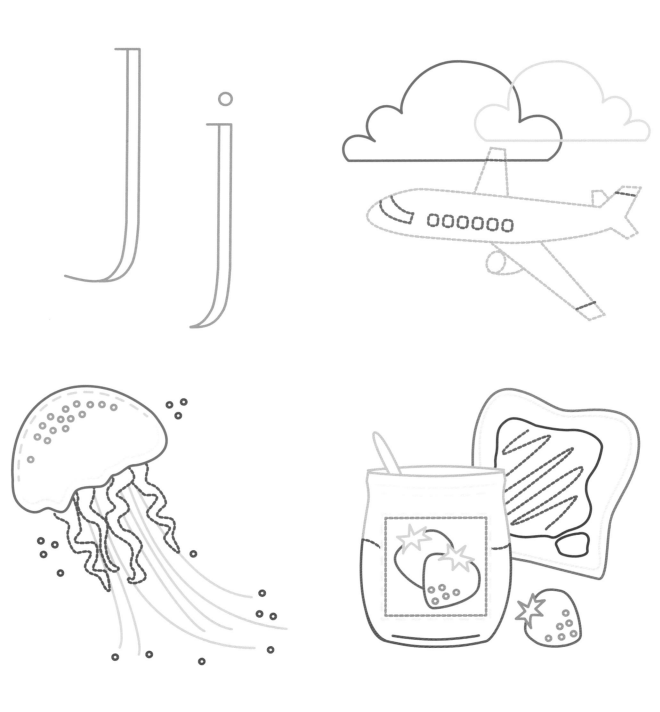

K k

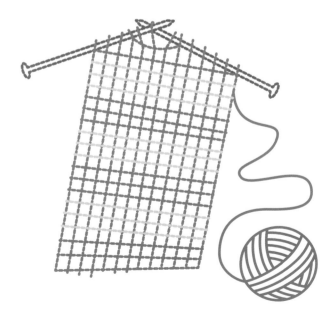

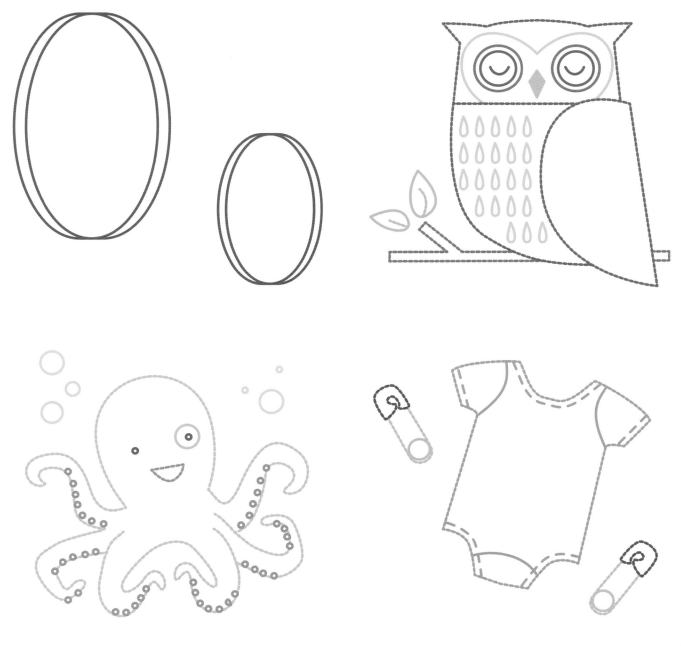

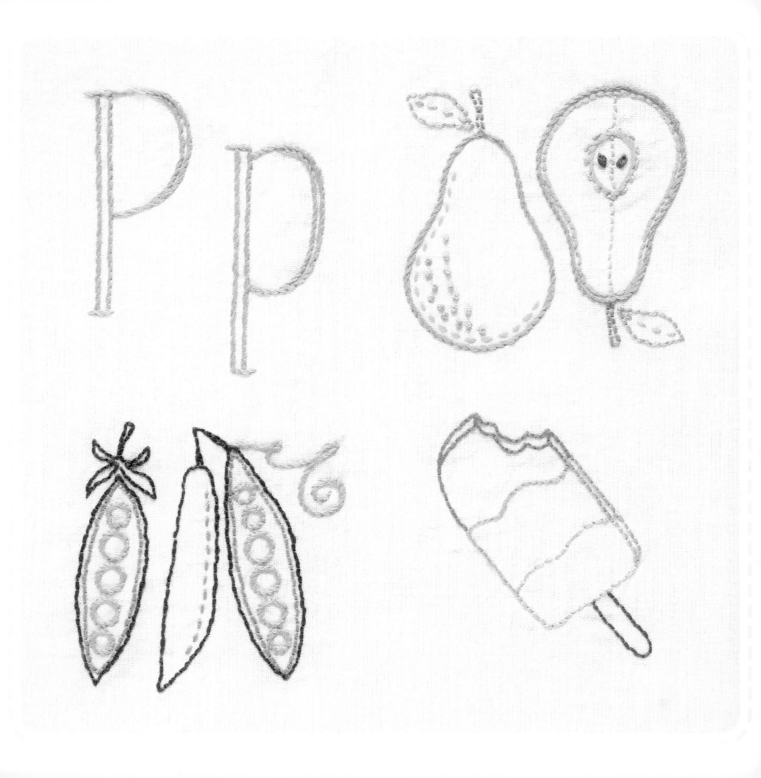

BE MINE